Soul Food: Feed Your Inspiration

Quotes and Inspirations to Feed What You Deeply Long For!

©2016

Soul Food: Feed Your Inspiration Quotes and Inspirations to Feed What You Deeply Long For!
Copyright ©2016 Bootstrap Businessmen

FREE eBOOK

Are you tired of doing the same ol' daily grind only to collect a paycheck and watch life pass you by? Wouldn't you like to chase your dreams and get paid for your passion? Won't you love to live life on your terms?

Then, the *8 Secrets to Turn Your Hobby into a Business* has your answers!

Bootstrap Businessmen hosts Dale L. Roberts and Kevin S. Allen compiled the best information on transitioning from passion to professional. The short report has simply, actionable steps anyone can use to direct their life toward greener pastures.

Go to Free.BootstrapBusinessmen.com
for your free report TODAY!

Soul Food: Feed Your Inspiration
Quotes and Inspirations to Feed What You Deeply Long For!

What you are longing for deep inside!
Before You Get Started Reading

We all need inspiration at some point in our lives, if you are starting a Business or going through a dark moment in your life. Please find the Pages filled with words and inspiration from some of the worlds greatest minds.

Twenty years from now you will be more disappointed by the things that you didn't do than by the ones you did do, so throw off the bowlines, sail away from safe harbor, catch the trade winds in your sails. Explore, Dream, Discover.
-Mark Twain

Too many of us are not living our dreams because we are living our fears.
-Les Brown, author, motivational speaker

If you can dream it, you can achieve it.

-Zig Ziglar, author, motivational speaker

Vision without action is daydream. Action without vision is nightmare.
-Japanese Proverb

You can't put a limit on anything. The more you dream, the farther you get.
-Michael Phelps, American Olympic swimmer

One of the most tragic things I know about human nature is that all of us tend to put off living. We are all dreaming of some magical rose garden over the horizon-instead of enjoying the roses blooming outside our windows today.
-Dale Carnegie, author, motivational speaker

At first dreams seem impossible, then improbable, then inevitable.
-Christopher Reeve, actor, author, activist

Don't be afraid of the space between your dreams and reality. If you can dream it, you can make it so.
-Belva Davis, TV and radio journalist

No dream is ever too small; no dream is ever too big.
-unknown source

Never let your memories be greater than your dreams.
-Doug Ivester, CEO of Coca-Cola

You will not do incredible things without an incredible dream.
-John Eliot

Don't be pushed by your problems; be led by your dreams.
-Ralph Waldo Emerson, writer

You are never too old to set another goal or to dream a new dream.
-Les Brown, author, motivational speaker

Every second you spend thinking about someone else's dreams you take time away from your own.
-Yogi Ramen

When we are motivated by goals that have deep meaning, by dreams that need completion, by pure love that needs expressing, then we truly live life.
-Greg Anderson

Build your own dreams, or someone else will hire you to build theirs.
-Farrah Gray, author, motivational speaker

The only thing that stands between you and your dream is the will to try and the belief that it is actually possible.
-Joel Brown

Keep away from people who try to belittle your dreams. Small people always do that, but the really great ones make you feel that you, too, can become great.
-Mark Twain

There are some people who live in a dream world, and there are some who face reality; and then there are those who turn one into the other.
-Douglas Everett

All men dream, but not equally. Those who dream by night in the dusty recesses of their minds wake in the day to find that it was vanity: but the dreamers of the day are dangerous men, for they may act their dreams with open eyes, to make it possible.
-T. E. Lawrence, archaeologist, British Army officer

The timing rarely seems "right" until we're looking back. Stop making excuses for your dreams.

-unknown source

Surround yourself with people who believe in your dreams.
-unknown source

Dreams don't work unless you do.
-John C. Maxwell, author, leadership expert

Devote yourself to an idea. Go make it happen. Struggle on it. Overcome your fears. Smile. Don't forget - this is your dream.
-unknown source

Dream as if you'll live forever. Live as if you'll die tomorrow.
-James Dean, actor

If your dreams don't scare you, they're not big enough.
-unknown source

All our dreams can come true if we have the courage to pursue them.
-Walt Disney

Take up one idea. Make that one idea your life - think of it, dream of it, live on that idea. Let the brain, muscles, nerves, every part of your body, be full of that idea, and just leave every other idea alone. This is the way to success.
-Swami Vivekananda, Indian Hindu monk

To accomplish great things, we must not only act, but also dream, not only plan, but also believe.
-Anatole France, writer

Some people dream of great things, while others stay awake and do them!
-unknown source

Successful people just focus on the task at hand. They don't dream too, too much. It's about executing the next step, and the next. One day you look up and you've climbed a mountain.
-Pat Larsen

You have to do what you dream of doing even while you're afraid.
-Arianna Huffington, writer

Dreaming isn't enough to see concrete achievements realized; talent isn't enough. The work you do is the main way to reach for your dreams. So act!
-Kristina Bazan

Never give up on a dream just because of the time it will take to accomplish it. The time will pass anyway.
-Earl Nightingale, self-help author

Who looks outside, dreams; who looks inside, awakes.
-Carl Gustav Jung, Swiss psychiatrist, psychotherapist

By recording your dreams and goals on paper, you set in motion the process of becoming the person you most want to be. Put your future in good hands - your own.
-Mark Victor Hansen, author

If you can imagine it, you can achieve it; if you can dream it, you can become it.
-William Arthur Ward, author

Study while others are sleeping; work while others are loafing; prepare while others are playing; and dream while others are wishing.
-William Arthur Ward, author

There are those who look at things the way they are, and ask why. I dream of things that never were, and ask why not?
-Robert Kennedy, American politician

Go confidently in the direction of your dreams. Live the life you have imagined.
-Henry David Thoreau, author, philosopher

Hope is a waking dream.
-Aristotle, Greek philosopher

Dream big and dare to fail.
-Norman D. Vaughan, American dogsled driver, explorer

Cherish your visions and your dreams as they are the children of your soul, the blueprints of your ultimate achievements.
-Napoleon Hill, author

A #2 pencil and a dream can take you anywhere.
-Joyce Meyer, Christian speaker and author

The best dreams happen when you're awake.
-Cherie Gilderbloom

No amount of security is worth the suffering of a mediocre life chained to a routine that has killed your dreams.
-unknown source

Now is the operative word. Everything you put in your way is just a method of putting off the hour when you could actually be doing your dream. You don't need endless time and perfect conditions. Do it now. Do it today. Do it for twenty minutes and watch your heart start beating.
-Barbara Sher, author, lifestyle coach

If one dream should fall and break into a thousand pieces, never be afraid to pick one of those pieces up and begin again.
-Flavia Weedn, author

Happiness consists in realizing it is all a great strange dream.
-Jack Kerouac, writer

Dreaming, after all, is a form of planning.
-Gloria Steinem, American feminist, social and political activist

Motivation is when your dreams put on work clothes.
-Benjamin Franklin

Never give up on your dream, because you never know what the Lord can bless you with.
-Kelly Rowland, musician

My parents taught me to never give up and to always believe that my future could be whatever I dreamt it to be.
-Susana Martinez, American politician

Never give up on what you really want to do. The person with big dreams is more powerful than the one with all the facts.
-H. Jackson Brown, Jr., author

Failing to follow after (our) dreams is one of the biggest life regrets we have today.
-unknown source

Goals are dreams with deadlines.
-Diana Scharf Hunt, author

The secret to productive goal setting is in establishing clearly defined goals, writing them down and then focusing on them several times a day with words, pictures and emotions as if we've already achieved them.
-Denis Waitley, author, motivational speaker

People with goals succeed because they know where they are going... It's as simple as that.
-Earl Nightingale, self-help author

We must walk consciously only part way toward our goal and then leap in the dark to our success.
-Henry David Thoreau, author, philosopher

First, have a definite, clear practical ideal; a goal, an objective. Second, have the necessary means to achieve your ends; wisdom, money, materials, and methods. Third, adjust all your means to that end.
-Aristotle, philosopher

What you get by achieving your goals is not as important as what you become by achieving your goals.
-Henry David Thoreau, author, philosopher

Obstacles are those frightful things you see when you take your eyes off your goal.
-Henry Ford

When defeat comes, accept it as a signal that your plans are not sound, rebuild those plans, and set sail once more toward your coveted goal.
-Napoleon Hill, author

Your goals are the road maps that guide you and show you what is possible for your life.
-Les Brown, author, motivational speaker

You are never too old to set another goal or to dream a new dream.
-Les Brown

In life, as in football, you won't go far unless you know where the goalposts are.
-Arnold H. Glasgow

When we are motivated by goals that have deep meaning, by dreams that need completion, by pure love that needs expressing, then we truly live life.
-Greg Anderson

The most important thing about goals is having one.
-Geoffrey F. Abert, author

The trouble with not having a goal is that you can spend your life running up and down the field and never score.
-Bill Copeland

You need a plan to build a house. To build a life, it is even more important to have a plan or goal.
-Zig Ziglar

The tragedy of life doesn't lie in not reaching your goal. The tragedy lies in having no goals to reach.
-Benjamin Mays

People with clear, written goals accomplish far more in a shorter period of time than people without them can ever imagine.
-Brian Tracy, author, motivational speaker

I think education is power. I think that being able to communicate with people is power. One of my main goals on the planet is to encourage people to empower themselves.
-Oprah Winfrey

Nothing can stop the man with the right mental attitude from achieving his goal.
-Thomas Jefferson

Winners compare their achievements with their goals, while losers compare their achievements with those of other people.
-Nido Qubein, motivational speaker, businessman

A goal without a plan is just a wish.
-Larry Elder, American radio and TV personality

You measure the size of the accomplishment by the obstacles you had to overcome to reach your goals.
-Booker T. Washington, author, orator, advisor to U.S. Presidents

Set your goals high, and don't stop till you get there.
-Bo Jackson, American pro athlete

Complaining does not work as a strategy. We all have finite time and energy. Any time we spend whining is unlikely to help us achieve our goals. And it won't make us happier.
-Randy Pausch

The tragedy in life doesn't lie in not reaching your goal. The tragedy lies in having no goal to reach.
-Benjamin Mays, American social activist

By recording your dreams and goals on paper, you set in motion the process of becoming the person you most want to be. Put your future in good hands - your own.
-Mark Victor Hansen, author

Desire is the key to motivation, but it's determination and commitment to an unrelenting pursuit of your goal - a commitment to excellence - that will enable you to attain the success you seek.

-Mario Andretti, racing driver

It is a paradoxical but profoundly true and important principle of life that the most likely way to reach a goal is to be aiming not at that goal itself but at some more ambitious goal beyond it.
-Arnold Toynbee, British historian, philosopher

You cannot expect to achieve new goals or move beyond your present circumstances unless you change.
-Les Brown, author, motivational speaker

Your goals, minus your doubts, equal your reality.
-Ralph Marston

You must have long-range goals to keep you from being frustrated by short-range failures.
-Charles C. Noble

If what you are doing is not moving you towards your goals, then it's moving you away from your goals.
-Brian Tracy, author, motivational speaker

This one step - choosing a goal and sticking to it - changes everything.
-Ishmael Scott Reed, writer, musician

The most important key to achieving great success is to decide upon your goal and launch, get started, take action, move.
-John Wooden, American basketball player and UCLA coach

You can't do it all yourself. Don't be afraid to rely on others to help you accomplish your goals.
-Oprah Winfrey

There is no such thing as a self-made man. You will reach your goals only with the help of others.
-George Shinn, former owner of various sports teams

Most of us, swimming against the tides of trouble the world knows nothing about, need only a bit of praise or encouragement - and we will make the goal.
-Jerome Fleishman, author

My goal when I come in here everyday is to make sure that if someone beats me - its not because they outworked me!
-Dr. Layne Norton, bodybuilder

The important thing is to strive towards a goal which is not immediately visible. That goal is not the concern of the mind, but of the spirit.
-Antoine de Saint-Exupéry, writer, pioneering aviator

The road leading to a goal does not separate you from the destination; it is essentially a part of it.
-Charles DeLint, writer

We are kept from our goal not by obstacles, but by a clear path to a lesser goal.
-Robert Brault, musician

Arriving at one goal is the starting point to another.
-John Dewey, American philosopher, psychologist

Most "impossible" goals can be met simply by breaking them down into bite size chunks, writing them down, believing them, and then going full speed ahead as if they were routine.
-Don Lancaster, author, inventor

Your goal should be just out of reach, but not out of sight.
-Denis Waitley, author, motivational speaker

Some men give up their designs when they have almost reached the goal; while others, on the contrary, obtain a victory by exerting, at the last moment, more vigorous efforts than before.
-Herodotus, Greek historian

It is not enough to take steps which may some day lead to a goal; each step must be itself a goal and a step likewise.
-Johann Wolfgang von Goethe, German writer and statesman

In absence of clearly defined goals, we become strangely loyal to performing daily acts of trivia.
-unknown source

So, it was a thing that my mother always taught me to go for your goals and never give up no matter what they are, and I started believing that later on in life.
-Michael Clarke Duncan, actor

I will keep smiling, be positive and never give up! I will give 100 percent each time I play. These are always my goals and my attitude.
-Yani Tseng, pro golfer

So many people will tell you "no", and you need to find something you believe in so hard that you just smile and tell them "watch me". Learn to take rejection as motivation to prove people wrong. Be unstoppable. Refuse to give up, no matter what. It's the best skill you can ever learn.
-Charlotte Eriksson, author, musician

Motivation alone is not enough. If you have an idiot and you motivate him, now you have a motivated idiot.

-Jim Rohn

People often say that motivation doesn't last. Well, neither does bathing. That's why we recommend it daily.
-Zig Ziglar, motivational speaker, author

The problem, often not discovered until late in life, is that when you look for things in life like love, meaning, motivation, it implies they are sitting behind a tree or under a rock. The most successful people in life recognize, that in life they create their own love, they manufacture their own meaning, they generate their own motivation. For me, I am driven by two main philosophies, know more today about the world than I knew yesterday. And lessen the suffering of others. You'd be surprised how far that gets you.
-Neil deGrasse Tyson, author, astrophysicist

Motivation is a fire from within. If someone else tries to light that fire under you, chances are it will burn very briefly.
-Stephen R. Covey, author, keynote speaker

I didn't believe in team motivation. I believe in getting a team prepared so it knows it will have the necessary confidence when it steps on the field and be prepared to play a good game.
-Tom Landry, former NFL coach

Ability is what you're capable of doing. Motivation determines what you do. Attitude determines how well you do it.
-Lou Holtz, college football analyst, former football coach

No one is going to tell you to get off your butt and work out. Motivation comes from within. No one wants this more than you.
-unknown source

In my experience, there is only one motivation, and that is desire. No reasons or principle contain it or stand against it.
-Jane Smiley, Pulitzer Prize-winning author

Motivation is like food for the brain. You cannot get enough in one sitting. It needs continual and regular refills.
-Peter Davies, author

Words embody power to inspire or motivate us, but it is only we who have power to open up to see and feel it.
-Anuj Somany, inspirational quotes writer

Motivation is when your dreams put on work clothes.
-Benjamin Franklin

You can motivate by fear, and you can motivate by reward. But both those methods are only temporary. The only lasting thing is self motivation.
-Homer Rice, former football player and coach

The greatest motivational act one person can do for another is to listen.
-Roy E. Moody, motivational speaker

Motivation is everything. You can do the work of two people, but you can't be two people. Instead, you have to inspire the next.
-Lee Iacocca, American businessman of the car industry

Motivation is an external, temporary high that pushes you forward. Inspiration is a sustainable internal glow which pulls you forward.
-Thomas Leonard, personal coaching expert

Striving for excellence motivates you; striving for perfection is demoralizing.
-Harriet Braiker, author

A creative man is motivated by the desire to achieve, not by the desire to beat others.
-Ayn Rand, writer, philosopher

To succeed, you need to find something to hold on to, something to motivate you, something to inspire you.
-Tony Dorsett, former NFL athlete

How to gain, how to keep, how to recover happiness is, in fact, for most men at all times the secret motive of all they do.
-William James, American philosopher and psychologist

Motivation is simple. You eliminate those who are not motivated.
-Lou Holtz, college football analyst, former football coach

Be miserable. Or motivate yourself. Whatever has to be done, it's always your choice.
-Dr. Wayne Dyer, motivational speaker, best-selling author

Heart in champions has to do with the depth of your motivation and how well your mind and body react to pressure - that is being able to do what you do best under maximum pain and stress.
-Bill Russell, former NBA athlete and coach

You don't have to be a fantastic hero to do certain things to compete. You can be just an ordinary person, sufficiently motivated to reach challenging goals.
-Sir Edmund Hillary, New Zealand mountaineer, explorer, philanthropist

Action must come first, and motivation comes later on.
-David Burns, professor emeritus in the Department of Psychiatry and Behavioral Sciences at the Stanford University School of Medicine, best-selling author

Without a compelling cause, our employees are just putting in time. Their minds might be engaged, but their hearts are not. Meaning precedes motivation.
-Lee J. Colan, author

Motivation is what gets you started. Habit is what keeps you going.
-Jim Ryun, American track & field Olympian

Virtually everyone needs motivation of some sort, but when you are in love - that is motivation enough, it turns many into poets and painters, it spurs the creativity in you.
-Bernard Kelvin Clive, author, speaker

Truth adds strength to our mind, courage to our heart, happiness to our soul and empowerment, motivation and inspiration to feel the best in our enriching life.
-Anuj Somany

It is not so much where my motivation comes from but rather how it manages to survive.
-Louise Bourgeois, artist

Desire is the key to motivation. It is the key to develop a healthy personality and a positive attitude towards oneself and others.
-Dr. Amit Abraham, author, psychologist

Needs cause motivation. Deep-rooted desires for esteem, affection,
belonging, achievement, self-actualization, power, and control motivate us to push for what we want and need in our lives.
-Lorii Myers, author, entrepreneur

If you truly feel that self esteem and motivation have to happen first before you can make changes in your life, then we'll probably be sharing walkers at a retirement home as we talk over what might have been.
-Shannon L. Alder, author

Success is not final and failure is not forever: it is the motivation we to choose that matters most.
-Lolly Daskal, writer, leadership expert

Motivation is not a lasting thing you can simply give to others unless they want it. Neither can I or anyone else give it to you unless you want it.
-Robin Nixon, author

Motivation will almost always beat mere talent.
-Norman Ralph Augustine, U.S. Aerospace businessman

No matter how good you are at planning, the pressure never goes away. So I don't fight it. I feed off it. I turn pressure into motivation to do my best
-Benjamin Carson, author, retired neurosurgeon

Wanting something is not enough. You must hunger for it. Your motivation must be absolutely compelling in order to overcome the obstacles that will invariably come your way.
-Les Brown, author, motivational speaker

Money is not a motivating factor for me. Money doesn't thrill me or make me play better because there are benefits to being wealthy. I'm just happy with a ball at my feet. My motivation comes from playing the game I love. If I wasn't being paid to be a professional footballer I would willingly play for nothing.
-Lionel Messi, Argentinian pro footballer

When you look at the people who are successful, you will find that they aren't the people who are motivated, but have consistency in their motivation.
-Arsene Wenger, French football manager, former footballer

I'll always use the negativity as more motivation to work even harder and become even stronger.
-Tim Tebow, NFL athlete

There's always the motivation of wanting to win. Everybody has that. But a champion needs, in his attitude, a motivation above and beyond winning.
-Pat Riley, former NBA coach and player

Once something is a passion, the motivation is there.
-Michael Schumacher, German retired racing driver

I grew up when I was 15 when I had my first opportunity in movies. I watched every great movie for a year and a half, and since then I have asked myself how I can emulate such artistry. That's really my motivation. I want to do something as good as my heroes have done.
-Leonardo DiCaprio, actor

One very important aspect of motivation is the willingness to stop and to look at things that no one else has bothered to look at. This simple process of focusing on things that are normally taken for granted is a powerful source of creativity.
-Edward de Bono, author, inventor, physician

I think it all comes down to motivation. If you really want to do something, you will work hard for it.
-Sir Edmund Hillary, New Zealand mountaineer, explorer, philanthropist

I'm not the type to pat myself on the back and all that, but somebody has to be lucky, right? When I got to Dallas, I was struggling - sleeping on the floor with six guys in a three-bedroom apartment. I used to drive around, look at the big houses, and imagine what it would be like to live there and use that as motivation.
-Mark Cuban, American businessman, 2014 Forbes list of wealthiest Americans

Other people's success spurs me on to do well and gives me motivation.
-Nicholas Hoult, actor

Success is knowing your purpose in life, growing to reach your maximum potential, and sowing seeds that benefit others.
-John C. Maxwell, author, leadership expert

I believe that what woman resents is not so much giving herself in pieces as giving herself purposelessly.
-Anne Morrow Lindbergh, author, aviator, wife of Charles Lindbergh

Everyone has a purpose in life. Perhaps yours is watching television.
-David Letterman, late night talk show host

The only true happiness comes from squandering ourselves for a purpose.
-William Cowper, English poet

Nothing contributes so much to tranquilizing the mind as a steady purpose - a point on which the soul may fix its intellectual eye.
-Mary Shelley, author

Many persons have a wrong idea of what constitutes true happiness. It is not attained through self-gratification but through fidelity to a worthy purpose.
-Helen Keller, American author, political activist, lecturer

The secret of success is constancy to purpose.
-Benjamin Disraeli, British Conservative politician, writer

This is our purpose: to make as meaningful as possible this life that has been bestowed upon us; to live in such a way that we may be proud of ourselves; to act in such a way that some part of us lives on.
-Oswald Spengler, German historian, philosopher

Unless a life is activated by sustained purpose it can become a depressingly haphazard affair.

-Richard Guggenheimer, painter

The real distinction is between those who adapt their purposes to reality and those who seek to mold reality in the light of their purposes.
-Henry Kissinger, American diplomat, political scientist

Man, unlike the animals, has never learned that the sole purpose of life is to enjoy it.
-Samuel Butler, English author

To want to be what one can be is purpose in life.
-Cynthia Ozick, author

My purpose in life does not include a hankering to charm society.
-James Dean, actor

I cannot believe that the purpose of life is (merely) to be happy. I think the purpose of life is to be useful, to be honorable, to be compassionate. I think it is above all to matter, to count, to stand for something. To have it make some difference that you lived at all.
-Leo Rosten, writer

To display the greatest powers, unless they are applied to great purposes, makes nothing for the character of greatness.
-William Hazlitt, English writer

Happiness is the meaning and the purpose of life, the whole aim and end of human existence.
-Aristotle, Greek philosopher

Great minds have purposes, others have wishes.
-Washington Irving, author

As long as anyone believes that his ideal and purpose is outside him, that it is above the clouds, in the past or in the future, he will go outside himself and seek fulfillment where it cannot be found. He will look for solutions and answers at every point except where they can be found-in himself.
-Erich Frohm, psychologist, philosopher

Firmness of purpose is one of the most necessary sinews of character, and one of the best instruments of success. Without it genius wastes its efforts in a maze of inconsistencies.
-Philip Dormer Chesterfield, British statesman

Thoughts lead on to purposes; purposes go forth in action; actions form habits; habits decide character; and character fixes our destiny.
-Tyron Edwards, American theologian

A purpose is the eternal condition of success.
-T. T. Munger, writer

Great minds have purposes, others have wishes. Little minds are tamed and subdued by misfortune; but great minds rise above them.
-Washington Irving, author

The man without a purpose is like a ship without a rudder - of, a nothing, a no man. Have a purpose in life, and, having it, throw such strength of mind and muscle into your work as God has given you.
-Thomas Carlyle, Scottish philosopher, writer

To begin to think with purpose, is to enter the ranks of those strong ones who only recognize failure as one of the pathways to attainment.
-James Allen, British philosophical writer

Nothing can resist the human will that will stake even its existence on its stated purpose.
-Benjamin Disraeli, British Conservative politician, writer

The purpose of life is a life of purpose.
-Robert Byrne, author

To come to be you must have a vision of Being, a Dream, a Purpose, a Principle. You will become what your vision is.
-Peter Nivio Zarlenga, author

The purpose of our lives is to be happy.
-Dalai Lama

We are all visitors to this time, this place. We are just passing through. Our purpose here is to observe, to learn, to grow, to love...and then we return home.
-Australian Aboriginal Proverb

Definiteness of purpose is the starting point of all achievement.
-W. Clement Stone, author, philanthropist

I am here for a purpose and that purpose is to grow into a mountain, not to shrink to a grain of sand. Henceforth will I apply all my efforts to become the highest mountain of all and I will strain my potential until it cries for mercy.
-Og Mandino, author

The meaning of life is to find your gift. The purpose of life is to give it away.
-Pablo Picasso

There is one quality that one must possess to win, and that is definiteness of purpose, the knowledge of what one wants, and a burning desire to possess it.
-Napoleon Hill, author

Decide upon your major definite purpose in life and then organize all your activities around it.
-Brian Tracy, motivational speaker, author

The successful person has the habit of doing the things failures don't like to do. They don't like doing them either necessarily. But their disliking is subordinated to the strength of their purpose.
-Albert E. N. Gray, author

The great and glorious masterpiece of man is to know how to live to purpose.
-Michel de Montaigne, philosopher of the French Renaissance

However brilliant an action may be, it should not be accounted great when it is not the result of a great purpose.
-Francois de la Rochefoucauld, author

Find a purpose in life so big it will challenge every capacity to be at your best.
-David O. McKay, ninth president of The Church of Jesus Christ of Latter-day Saints

Success demands singleness of purpose.
-Vincent Lombardi, American football player, coach and executive

The only failure one should fear, is not hugging to the purpose they see as best.
-George Eliot, English writer

Happiness comes when we test our skills towards some meaningful purpose.
-John Stossel, TV personality, author

Patience and tenacity of purpose are worth more than twice their weight of cleverness.
-Thomas Henry Huxley, English biologist

You are only as strong as your purpose, therefore let us choose reasons to act that are big, bold, righteous and eternal.
-Barry Munro

The successful men of today are men of one overmastering idea, one unwavering aim, men of single and intense purpose.
-Orison Swett Marden, author

Singleness of purpose is one of the chief essentials for success in life, no matter what may be one's aim.

-John D. Rockefeller

Efforts and courage are not enough without purpose and direction.
-John F Kennedy

You can come to understand your purpose in life by slowing down and feeling your heart's desires.
-Marcia Wieder, author, keynote speaker

The most distinguishing feature of winners is their intensity of purpose.
-Alymer Letterman

The great and glorious masterpiece of man is how to live with purpose.
-Michel de Montaigne , French philosopher

Energy is equal to desire and purpose.
-Sheryl Adams

Do not, for one repulse, forego the purpose that you resolved to effect.
-William Shakespeare

Resistance is a powerful motivator precisely because it enables us to fulfill our longing to achieve our goals while letting us boldly recognize and name the obstacles to those achievements.
-Derrick A. Bell, author

Strong lives are motivated by dynamic purposes.
-Kenneth Hildebrand

Strength is the product of struggle. You must do what others don't to achieve what others won't.
-Henry Rollins, musician, actor, speaker

Strength does not come from physical capacity. It comes from an indomitable will.
-Mahatma Gandhi

You gain strength, courage and confidence by every experience in which you stop to look fear in the face.
-Eleanor Roosevelt, politician, diplomat, activist

The pain you feel today is the strength you feel tomorrow. For every challenge encountered there is opportunity for growth.
-Ritu Ghatourey, writer

Strength of character means the ability to overcome resentment against others, to hide hurt feelings, and to forgive quickly.
-Ritu Ghatourey, writer

Difficulties strengthen the mind, as labor does the body.
-Lucius Annaeus Seneca, Roman Stoic philosopher

We must train from the inside out. Using our strengths to attack and nullify any weaknesses. It's not about denying a weakness may exist but about denying its right to persist.
-Vince McConnell

Do not pray for an easy life, pray for the strength to endure a difficult one.
-Bruce Lee, actor, martial arts expert, philosopher

Do not ask for less responsibility to be free and relaxed—ask for more strength.
-Sheng Yen, religious scholar, teacher

Our strength grows out of our weaknesses.
-Ralph Waldo Emerson, 19th century American essayist, lecturer, and poet

Strong is what happens when you run out of weak.
-unknown source

Enter every activity without giving mental recognition to the possibility of defeat. Concentrate on your strengths instead of your weaknesses, on your powers instead of your problems.
-Paul J. Meyer, personal development expert, author, speaker

When I dare to be powerful - to use my strength in the service of my vision, then it becomes less and less important whether I am afraid.
-Audre Lorde, writer, civil rights activist

My attitude is that if you push me towards something that you think is a weakness, then I will turn that perceived weakness into a strength.
-Michael Jordan, former professional basketball player, entrepreneur

Character cannot be developed in ease and quiet. Only through experience of trial and suffering can the soul be strengthened, ambition inspired, and success achieved.
-Helen Keller, American author, political activist, lecturer

Life is very interesting. In the end, some of your greatest pains become your greatest strengths.
-Drew Barrymore, actress, producer/director, author

Stand up to your obstacles and do something about them. You will find that they haven't half the strength you think they have.

-Norman Vincent Peale, author, minister

Worry does not empty tomorrow of its sorrow; it empties today of its strength.
-Corrie ten Boom, Dutch Christian who helped many Jews escape the Nazi Holocaust during World War II

The turning point in the process of growing up is when you discover the core of strength within you that survives all hurt.
-Max Lerner, journalist, educator

Everyone should carefully observe which way his heart draws him, and then choose that way with all his strength.
-Hasidic saying

Life only demands from you the strength you possess. Only one feat is possible—not to have run away.
-Dag Hammarskjold, Swedish diplomat, author

Look for strengths in people, not weakness; for good, not evil. Most of us find what we search for.
-J. Wilbur Chapman, 19th century Presbyterian evangelist

The undertaking of a new action brings new strength.
-Evenius, Ancient Greek legendary seer

Let me tell you the secret that has led me to my goal. My strength lies solely in my tenacity.
-Louis Pasteur, French chemist, microbiologist, renowned for his discoveries of the principles of vaccination, microbial fermentation and pasteurization

Look well into thyself; there is a source of strength which will always spring up if thou wilt always look there.
-Marcus Aurelius Antoninus, Roman Emperor

The real man smiles in trouble, gathers strength from distress, and grows brave by reflection.
-Thomas Paine, 18th century philosopher, political activist, revolutionary

Only actions give life strength; only moderation gives it a charm.
-Jean Paul Richter, German Romantic writer (late 18th to early 19th century)

Conquering others takes force, conquering yourself is true strength.
-Lao-Tzu, Ancient China philosopher, poet

Three failures denote uncommon strength. A weakling has not enough grit to fail thrice.
-Minna Thomas Antrim, American writer

I was always looking outside myself for strength and confidence, but it comes from within. It is there all the time.
-Anna Freud, psychoanalyst, daughter of Sigmund Freud, pioneer of psychoanalysis

We confide in our strength, without boasting of it; we respect that of others, without fearing it.
-Thomas Jefferson, American Founding Father, 3rd U.S. President

True strength lies in gentleness.
-Irish Proverb

He knows not his own strength that hath not met adversity.
-Ben Jonson, 17th century English dramatist, poet

Few men during their lifetime come anywhere near exhausting the resources dwelling within them. There are deep wells of strength that are never used.
-Richard Byrd, pioneering American aviator, polar explorer

Tenderness and kindness are not signs of weakness and despair, but manifestations of strength and resolutions.
-Kahlil Gibran, Lebanese artist, writer, poet

People do not lack strength, they lack will.
-Victor Hugo, French poet, novelist, dramatist of the Romantic movement

Greatness lies not in being strong, but in the right use of strength.
-Henry Ward Beecher, American Congregationalist clergyman, social reformer, speaker

One who gains strength by overcoming obstacles possesses the only strength which can overcome adversity.
-Albert Schweitzer, OM, German theologian, philosopher, physician, medical missionary in Africa

Rudeness is the weak man's imitation of strength.
-Eric Hoffer, American moral and social philosopher, author

All the adversity I've had in my life, all my troubles and obstacles, have strengthened me. You may not realize it when it happens, but a kick in the teeth may be the best thing in the world for you.
-Walt Disney, American business magnate, cartoonist, animator, voice actor, film producer

Old age is not a disease- it is strength and survivorship, triumph over all kinds of vicissitudes and disappointments, trials and illnesses.
-Samuel Johnson, English writer, moralist, literary critic

He that wrestles with us strengthens our nerves and sharpens our skill. Our antagonist is our helper.
-Edmund Burke, Irish statesman, author, orator and philosopher

To be capable of steady friendship or lasting love, are the two greatest proofs, not only of goodness of heart, but of strength.
-William Hazlitt, English writer, social commentator, philosopher

It is in the knowledge of the genuine conditions of our lives that we
must draw our strength to live and our reasons for living.
-Simone de Beauvoir, French writer, existentialist philosopher, political activist

Strength is a matter of the made-up mind.
-John Beecher, American activist poet, writer, journalist

On the edge of destiny, you must test your strength.
-Billy Bishop, Canadian First World War top flying ace credited with 72 victories

Strength does not come from physical capacity. It comes from an indomitable will.
-Mahatma Gandhi, preeminent leader of Indian independence movement in British-ruled India

It is a sign of strength, not of weakness, to admit that you don't know all the answers.
-John P. Loughrane, author
He turns all of his injuries into strengths, that which does not kill him makes him stronger, he is superman.
-Friedrich Nietzsche, 19th century German philologist, philosopher, poet

Our strength often increases in proportion to the obstacles imposed upon it.
-Paul De Rapin, French historian

Learn to think like a winner. Think positive and visualize your strengths.
-Vic Braden, American tennis player, instructor, television broadcaster

Our real problem is not our strength today; it is rather the vital necessity of action today to ensure our strength tomorrow.
-Dwight D. Eisenhower, 34th U.S. President

Nurture strength of spirit to shield you in sudden misfortune.
-Max Ehrmann, American writer, poet

If you haven't the strength to impose your own terms upon life, then you must accept the terms it offers you.
-T. S. Eliot, essayist, publisher, playwright, literary, social critic

You don't need strength to let go of something. What you really need is understanding.
-Guy Finley, American self-help writer, philosopher, and spiritual teacher

In the darkest hour the soul is replenished and given strength to continue and endure.
-Heart Warrior Chosa, author

Hard things are put in our way, not to stop us, but to call out our courage and strength.
-Victor Hugo, French poet, novelist, dramatist of the Romantic movement

Being deeply loved by someone gives you strength, loving someone deeply gives you courage.
-Lao Tzu, Ancient China philosopher, poet

Nothing great in the world has been accomplished without passion.
-Georg Wilhelm Friedrich Hegelm, 18th century German philosopher

I would rather die of passion than of boredom.
-Vincent van Gogh, 19th century Dutch artist

If what you're doing is not your passion, you have nothing to lose.
-Celestine Chua, personal development expert, author

Do it with passion or not at all. Wherever you go, go with all your heart.
-unknown source

Passion is pushing yourself when no one else is around.
-unknown source

Passion trumps everything.
-Dave Tate, fitness expert, author

Even if you know it's your passion, there will be things you won't like but you'll have to do regardless.
-unknown source

Never give up, have the passion. Don't be afraid.
-Barbara Broccoli, American film producer

Great dancers are not great because of their technique, they are great because of their passion.
-Martha Graham, American modern dancer, choreographer

Ambition is so powerful a passion in the human breast, that however high we reach we are never satisfied.

-Niccolo Machiavelli, Florentine historian, politician, diplomat, philosopher, writer during the Renaissance

The happiness of a man in this life does not consist in the absence but in the mastery of his passions.
-Alfred Lord Tennyson, 19th century Poet Laureate of Great Britain and Ireland

All human actions have one or more of these seven causes: chance, nature, compulsion, habit, reason, passion, and desire.
-Aristotle, Greek philosopher, scientist

Only passions, great passions, can elevate the soul to great things.
-Denis Diderot, 18th century French philosopher, art critic, writer

Clarity of mind means clarity of passion, too; this is why a great and clear mind loves ardently and sees distinctly what it loves.
-Blaise Pascal, 17th century French mathematician, physicist, inventor, writer, Christian philosopher

The worst sin - perhaps the only sin - passion can commit, is to be joyless.
-Dorothy L. Sayers, English crime writer, translator

You can overcome any obstacles by asking the right questions of the right people at the right time, then act on that advice with passion.
-Dan Surface, author

Absence extinguishes small passions and increases great ones, as the wind blows out a candle, and blows in a fire.
-François de la Rochefoucauld, 17th century French author

Every man without passions has within him no principle of action, nor motive to act.
-Claude A. Helvetius, 18th century French philosopher, freemason, literature expert

If we resist our passions, it is more from their weakness than from our strength.
-François de la Rochefoucauld, 17th century French author

Develop a passion for learning. If you do, you will never cease to grow.
-Anthony D'Angelo, American writer

Never let your persistence and passion turn into stubbornness and ignorance.
-Anthony D'Angelo, American writer

There is a boundary to men's passions when they act from feelings but none when they are under the influence of imagination.
-Edmund Burke, Irish statesman, author, orator, philosopher

Playing seems to be both disinterested and passionate at the same time disinterested in that it is not for real, and passionate in the absorption it requires.
-Oliver Bevan, English artist

Feeling passionate about something is like getting a peak at your soul smiling back at you.
-Amanda Medinger

Passion costs me too much to bestow it on every trifle.
-Thomas Adams, 19th-century American scientist, inventor

Passion is in all great searches and is necessary to all creative endeavors.
-W. Eugene Smith, American photojournalist

A strong passion will insure success, for the desire of the end will point out the means. -Willam Hazlitt, 18th to 19th century English writer, philosopher

The fastest way to pass your own expectations is to add passion to your labor.
-Mike Litman, author, motivational speaker

The three P's of success: Passion, Persistence, and Patience.
-Doug Bronson

Passion holds up the bottom of the universe and genius paints up its roof.
-Chao Chang

This is the art of courage: to see things as they are and still believe that the victory lies not with those who avoid the bad, but those who taste, in living awareness, every drop of the good.
-Victoria Lincoln, author

Courage is the first of human qualities because it is the quality which guarantees the others.
-Aristotle, Greek philosopher, scientist

You can never cross the ocean until you have the courage to lose sight of the shore.
-Christopher Columbus, Italian explorer, navigator, colonizer

Life shrinks or expands in proportion to one's courage.
-Anais Nin, author

Sometimes even to live is an act of courage.
-Lucius Annaeus Seneca, Roman Stoic philosopher, statesman, dramatist

To uncover your true potential, you must first find your own limits and then you have to have the courage to blow past them.
-Picabo Street, American former World Cup alpine ski racer, Olympic gold medalist

Your time is limited, so don't waste it living someone else's life. Don't be trapped by dogma - which is living with the results of other people's thinking. Don't let the noise of others' opinions drown out your own inner voice. And most importantly, have the courage to follow your heart and intuition. They somehow already know what you truly want to become. Everything else is secondary.
-Steve Jobs, American entrepreneur, marketer, inventor

You learn you can do your best even when it's hard, even when you're tired and maybe hurting a little bit. It feels good to show some courage.
-Joe Namath, former American football quarterback and actor

Courage doesn't always roar. Sometimes courage is the quiet voice at the end of the day saying, "I will try again tomorrow."
-Mary Anne Radmacher, author, artist

The miracle isn't that I finished. The miracle is that I had the courage to start.
-unknown source

Courage is the power of the mind to overcome fear.
-Martin Luther King, Jr., American Baptist minister, activist, humanitarian, leader in the African-American Civil Rights Movement

Courage is being scared to death - but saddling up anyway.
-John Wayne, American film actor, director and producer

Courage is fear holding on a minute longer.
-General George S. Patton, U.S. Army General

Courage is not the absence of fear, but rather the judgment that something else is more important than fear.
-Ambrose Redmoon, writer

It often requires more courage to dare to do right than to fear to do wrong.
-Abraham Lincoln, 16th U.S. President

It takes courage to grow up and become who you really are!
-E. E. Cummings, American poet, painter, essayist, author, and playwright

Success is not final, failure is not fatal: it is the courage to continue that counts.

-Winston Churchill, British Prime Minister

You can't test courage cautiously!
-Annie Dillard, American author

Whatever course you decide upon, there is always someone to tell you that you are wrong. There are always difficulties arising which tempt you to believe that your critics are right. To map out a course of action and follow it to an end requires courage.
–Ralph Waldo Emerson, 19th century American essayist, lecturer, and poet

God, grant me the serenity to accept the things I cannot change; courage to change the things I can; and wisdom to know the difference.
-Reinhold Niebuhr's The Serenity Prayer

Courage is the power to let go of the familiar.
-Raymond Lindquist

Do not lose courage in considering your own imperfections.
-Saint Francis de Sales, former Bishop of Geneva, honored as a saint in the Roman Catholic Church

Courage means going against majority opinion in the name of the truth.
-Válcav Havel, writer, philosopher, 1st democratically elected President of Czechoslovakia

When you meet your antagonist, do everything in a mild and
agreeable manner. Let your courage be as keen, but at the same time as polished, as your sword.
-Richard Brinsley Sheridan, 18th to 19th century Irish playwright and poet

Any intelligent fool can make things bigger and more complex...it takes a touch of genius - and a lot of courage - to move in the opposite direction.
-Albert Einstein, German-born theoretical physicist

Courage is contagious. When a brave man takes a stand, the spines of others are often stiffened.
-Billy Graham, American Christian evangelist

Courage is grace under pressure.
-Ernest Hemingway, American author and journalist

Everyone has talent. What is rare is the courage to follow talent to the dark place where it leads
-Erica Jong, American author and teacher

Courage and perseverance have a magical talisman, before which difficulties disappear and obstacles vanish into air.
-John Quincy Adams, 6th U.S. President

Have the courage to be ignorant of a great number of things, in order to avoid the calamity of being ignorant of everything.
-Sydney Smith, English writer, Anglican cleric

The secret of happiness is freedom, and the secret of freedom, courage.
-Thucydides, Athenian historian, political philosopher and general

Happiness is a form of courage.
-Holbrook Jackson, British journalist, writer, publisher

People grow through experience if they meet life honestly and courageously. This is how character is built.
-Eleanor Roosevelt, politician, diplomat, activist

The best weapons against the infamies of life are courage, willfulness and patience. Courage strengthens, willfulness is fun and patience provides tranquility.
-Hermann Hesse, German-born Swiss poet, novelist, painter

We must believe in ourselves or no one else will believe in us; we must match our aspirations with the competence, courage, and determination to succeed.
-Rosalyn Sussman Yalow, American medical physicist, co-winner of the 1977 Nobel Prize in Physiology/Medicine

All of our dreams can come true, if we have the courage to pursue them.
-Walt Disney, American business magnate, cartoonist, animator, voice actor, film producer

It requires more courage to suffer than to die.
-Napoleon Bonaparte, French military and political leader

Failure is unimportant. It takes courage to make a fool of yourself.
-Charlie Chaplin, English comic actor, filmmaker

What a new face courage puts on everything.
-Ralph Waldo Emerson, 19th century American essayist, lecturer, and poet

The greatest test of courage on earth is to bear defeat without losing heart.
-Robert G. Ingersoll, American lawyer, a Civil War veteran, political leader, and orator

Courage without conscience is a wild beast.
-Robert G. Ingersoll, American lawyer, a Civil War veteran, political leader, and orator

Courage is the ladder on which all other virtues mount.
-Clare Booth Luce, first American woman appointed to a major ambassadorial post abroad, author

It is from numberless diverse acts of courage and belief that human history is shaped.
-Robert F. Kennedy, American politician

Successful leaders have the courage to take action where others hesitate.
-John C. Maxwell, American author, speaker, pastor

Conscience is the root of all true courage; if a man would be brave let him obey his conscience.
-James F. Clarke, American theologian, author

There is nothing in the world so much admired as a man who knows how to bear unhappiness with courage.
-Lucius Annaeus Seneca, Roman Stoic philosopher, statesman, dramatist

True courage is not the brutal force of vulgar heroes, but the firm resolve of virtue and reason.
-Alfred North Whitehead, English mathematician, philosopher
He who does not have the courage to speak up for his rights cannot earn the respect of others.
-Ren G. Torres

The highest courage is to dare to appear to be what one is.
-John Lancaster Spalding, American author, poet, the first bishop of the Roman Catholic Diocese of Peoria from 1877 to 1908, co-founder of The Catholic University of America

Courage is the thing. All goes if courage goes.
-Joseph Addison, 17th - 18th Century English essayist, poet, statesman

The courage of life is often a less dramatic spectacle than the courage of a final moment but it is no less than a magnificent mixture of triumph and tragedy.
-John F. Kennedy, 35th U.S. President

What would life be if we had no courage to attempt anything?
-Vincent Van Gogh, 19th century Dutch artist

Courage is not simply one of the virtues, but the form of every virtue at the testing point.
-C.S. Lewis, novelist, broadcaster, lecturer

The only courage that matters is the kind that gets you from one moment to the next.
-Mignon McLaughlin, American journalist, author

The great virtue in life is real courage that knows how to face facts and live beyond them.

-D. H. Lawrence, English novelist, playwright, painter

Courage is the capacity to confront what can be imagined.
-Leo C. Rosten, Russian humorist writer

To bear failure with courage is the best proof of character that anyone can give.
-W. Somerset Maugham, British writer

Without courage you cannot practice any of the other virtues with consistency.
-Maya Angelou, American author, poet, dancer, actress, singer

One man scorned and covered with scars still strove with his last ounce of courage to reach the unreachable stars and the world.
-Miguel de Cervantes, Spanish novelist, poet, playwright

Courage and perseverance have a magical talisman, before which difficulties disappear and obstacles vanish into air.
-John Quincy Adams, 6th U.S. President

No one has yet computed how many imaginary triumphs are silently celebrated by people each year to keep up their courage.
-Athenaeus, 2nd to 3rd century Greek rhetorician, grammarian, author

The scars you acquire by exercising courage, will never make you feel inferior.
-D. A. Battista

Courage is more than standing for a firm conviction. It includes the risk of questioning that conviction.
-Julian Weber Gordon

We must have the courage to bet on our ideas, to take the calculated risk, and to act. Everyday living requires courage if life is to be effective and bring happiness.
-Maxwell Maltz, American author, cosmetic surgeon

As for courage and will - we cannot measure how much of each lies within us, we can only trust there will be sufficient to carry.
-Andre Norton, American writer

Courage consists not in blindly overlooking danger, but in seeing it, and conquering it.
-Jean Paul Friedrich Richter, German Romantic writer

Have patience with all things, but chiefly have patience with yourself. Do not lose courage in considering you own imperfections, but instantly set about remedying them - every day begin the task anew.

-Saint Francis de Sales, former Bishop of Geneva, honored as a saint in the Roman Catholic Church

Determination, patience and courage are the only things needed to improve any situation.
-unknown source

A man of courage flees forward in the midst of new things.
-Jacques Maritain, French Catholic philosopher

Courage is daring to take the first step, or a different path. It is the decision to place your dreams above your fears.
-unknown source

Courage can't see around corners, but goes around them anyway.
-Mignon McLaughlin, American journalist, author

You will never do anything in this world without courage. It is the greatest quality of the mind next to honor.
-James Allen, British philosophical writer

Vision plus desire equals reality. We must have courage to bet on our ideas, take the calculated risk, and take action.
-Martin Brown, Australian cartoonist/illustrator

If we are to survive, we must have ideas, vision, and courage. These things are rarely produced by committees.
-Arthur Schlesinger, American historian, social critic, public intellectual

Confidence is courage at ease.
-Daniel Maher

Ingenuity, plus courage, plus work, equals miracles.
-Bob Richards, U.S. Olympic athlete

Courage is reckoned the greatest of all virtues; because, unless a man has that virtue, he has no security for preserving any other.
-Samuel Johnson, English writer, moralist, literary critic

More powerful than the will to win is the courage to begin.
-unknown source

Deal honestly and objectively with yourself; intellectual honesty and personal courage are the hallmarks of great character.
-Brian Tracy, author, motivational speaker

Courage atrophies from lack of use.
-unknown source

Courage is very important. Like a muscle, it is strengthened by use.
-Ruth Gordon, American actress, screenwriter, playwright

When in doubt, do the courageous thing.
-Jan Smuts, South African & British Commonwealth statesman, military leader, philosopher

Hard things are put in our way, not to stop us, but to call out our courage and strength.
-unknown source

Powerful words come with powerful intent. Where you have passion, strength, courage, and determination you can accomplish anything.
-K.L. Toth, author, freelance journalist

Success without fulfillment is the ultimate failure.
-Tony Robbins

For true success ask yourself these four questions: Why? Why not? Why not me? Why not now?
-James Allen, 19th-20th century British philosophical author

Just know, when you truly want success, you'll never give up on it. No matter how bad the situation may get.
-unknown source

Did you ever notice those who criticize the strong or the elite are usually weaker or less successful than those they pass judgment on?
-Louie Simmons, American powerlifter and strength coach

A successful man is one who can lay a firm foundation with the bricks others have thrown at him.
-David Brinkley, American newscaster

Success does not consist in never making mistakes but in never making the same one a second time.
-George Bernard Shaw, Irish playwright, co-founder of the London School of Economics

Success is dependent upon the glands - sweat glands.
-Zig Ziglar, American author, salesman, motivational speaker

Success doesn't happen overnight. Keep your eyes on the prize and don't look back.

-Erin Andrews, American sportscaster, television personality

Overnight success is fictional. Overnight success comes after years of hard, sustainable work.
Andrew Dumont, blogger, entrepreneur

Success is not to be measured by the position someone has reached in life, but the obstacles he has overcome while trying to succeed.
-Booker T. Washington, African-American educator, author, orator, advisor to U.S. Presidents

Success is a function of persistence and doggedness and the willingness to work hard for twenty-two minutes to make sense of something that most people would give up on after thirty seconds.
-Malcolm Gladwell, Canadian journalist, bestselling author, speaker

We need to be continuously striving to go beyond our comfort zones if we want to be successful.
Heidi Grant Halvorson, social psychologist, speaker, author

Character cannot be developed in ease and quiet. Only through experience of trial and suffering can the soul be strengthened, ambition inspired, and success achieved.
-Helen Keller, American author, political activist, lecturer

Success is how high you bounce when you hit bottom.
-General George S. Patton, U.S. Army General

It's such a fine line between success or not, which makes the sweet moments that much more worth savoring.
-Nick Willis, U.S. 1500-meter Olympian, 2012

To be successful, you must decide exactly what you want to accomplish, then resolve to pay the price to get it.
-Bunker Hunt, American oil company executive

You don't become enormously successful without encountering some really interesting problems.
-Mark Victor Hansen, American motivational speaker, trainer, author

Success depends on your backbone, not your wishbone.
-unknown source

If you have no critics you'll likely have no success.
-Malcolm Forbes, American entrepreneur, publisher of Forbes magazine

Success seems to be largely a matter of hanging on after others have let go.

-William Feather, American publisher, author

When I thought I couldn't go on, I forced myself to keep going. My success is based on persistence, not luck.
-Norman Lear, American writer, television producer

If you are successful, you may win false friends and true enemies. Succeed anyway.
-Mother Theresa, Roman Catholic religious sister, missionary

I am not telling you that achieving success is going to be easy, I am telling you that it's going to be worth it!
-Art Williams, American insurance executive

Success demands that we learn to discipline our disappointment.
-Jim Rohn, American entrepreneur, author, motivational speaker

The toughest thing about success is that you've got to keep on being a success.
-Irving Berlin, Jewish-American composer, lyricist

Sweat plus sacrifice equals success.
-Charles O. Finley, American businessman, former owner of MLB Oakland Athletics

You must learn from your past mistakes, but not lean on your past successes.
-Denis Waitley, American motivational speaker, best-selling author

The successful man will profit from his mistakes and try again in a different way.
-Dale Carnegie, American writer, lecturer

You never know how close you are to victory or success, so keep pushing!
-Brian Tracy, American author, motivational speaker
Creating success is tough but keeping it is tougher.
-Pete Rose, former Major League Baseball player, manager

Through perseverance, many people win success out of what seemed destined to be certain failure.
-Benjamin Disraeli, British Prime Minister, conservative politician, writer

Most success springs from an obstacle or failure.
-Scott Adams, American cartoonist, author

Each success only buys an admission ticket to a more difficult problem.
-Henry Kissinger, American diplomat, political scientist

Instead of thinking about where you are, think about where you want to be. It takes twenty years of hard work to become an overnight success.
-Diana Rankin, life coach, keynote speaker

The test of a successful person is not an ability to eliminate all problems before they arise, but to meet and work out difficulties when they do arise.
-David J. Schwartz, American motivational writer, coach

How many a man has thrown up his hands at a time when a little more effort, a little more patience would have achieved success?
-Elbert Hubbard, American writer, publisher, artist, philosopher

Behind every successful man there are usually a lot of unsuccessful years.
-unknown source

The prospect of success in achieving our most cherished dream is not without its terrors. Who is more deprived and alone than the man who has achieved his dream?
-Brendan Behan, Irish poet, short story writer, novelist, playwright

The superior man makes the difficulty to be overcome his first interest; success only comes later.
-Confucius, Chinese teacher, editor, politician, philosopher

Always remember that striving and struggle precede success, even in the dictionary.
-Sarah Ban Breathnach, author

Formulate and stamp indelibly on your mind a mental picture of yourself as succeeding. Hold this picture tenaciously. Never permit it to fade. Your mind will seek to develop the picture...Do not build up obstacles in your imagination.
-Norman Vincent Peale, author, minister

Success consists of getting up just one more time than you fall.
-Oliver Goldsmith, Anglo-Irish novelist, playwright, poet

Failure is success if we learn from it.
-Malcolm Forbes, American entrepreneur, publisher

Failure is the condiment that gives success its flavor.
-Truman Capote, American author, screenwriter, playwright, actor

Develop success from failures. Discouragement and failure are two of the surest stepping stones to success.
-Dale Carnegie, American writer, lecturer

It is during our failures that we discover our true desire for success!
-Kevin Ngo, author

I'd rather be a failure at something I love than a success at something I hate.
-George Burns, American comedian, award-winning actor, best-selling writer

Success is never certain. Failure is never final.
-John Wooden, American basketball player, coach

Recovering from failure is often easier than building from success.
-Michael Eisner, American businessman, former-chief executive officer of The Walt Disney Company

If the truth be known, most successes are built on a multitude of failures.
-unknown source

A word of encouragement during a failure is worth more than an hour of praise after success.
-unknown source

Success is the ability to go from failure to failure without losing your enthusiasm.
-Sir Winston Churchill, British politician, Prime Minister

If you worry about yesterday's failures, then today's successes will be few.
-Brian Tracy, American author, motivational speaker

In order to succeed, your desire for success should be greater than your fear of failure.
-Bill Cosby, American stand-up comedian, actor, author, activist

Celebrate your success and find humor in your failures. Don't take yourself so seriously. Loosen up and everyone around you will loosen up. Have fun and always show enthusiasm. When all else fails, put on a costume and sing a silly song.
-Sam Walton, American businessman, entrepreneur, founder of Wal-Mart

Many of life's failures are people who did not realize how close they were to success when they gave up.
-Thomas Edison, American inventor, businessman

Failure is only a temporary change in direction to set you straight for your next success.
-Denis Waitley, American motivational speaker, best-selling author

The road to success and the road to failure are almost exactly the same.
-Colin R. Davis, English conductor

It takes as much stress to be a success as it does to be a failure.

-Emilio James Trujillo

The difference between failure and success is doing a thing nearly right and doing it exactly right.
-Edward Simmons, American Impressionist painter

The great dividing line between success and failure can be expressed in five words: I did not have time.
-unknown source

Many people dream of success. To me success can only be achieved through repeated failure and introspection.
-Soichiro Honda, Japanese engineer, industrialist

If you want to double your success rate, you need to double your failure rate.
-Thomas John Watson, Sr., American businessman

One fails forward toward success.
-Charles Kettering, American inventor, engineer, businessman, holder of 186 patents

Sometimes a noble failure serves the world as faithfully as a distinguished success.
-Edward Dowden, Irish critic, poet

Forget about the consequences of failure. Failure is only a temporary change in direction to set you straight for your next success.
-Denis Waitley, American motivational speaker, best-selling author

It's how you deal with failure that determines how you achieve success.
-David Feherty, former professional golfer

Failure is a prerequisite for great success. If you want to succeed faster, double your rate of failure.
-Brian Tracy, American author, motivational speaker

I have tried 99 times and have failed, but on the 100th time came success.
-Albert Einstein, German-born theoretical physicist

You become strong by defying defeat and by turning loss into gain and failure to success.
-Napoleon Hill, American author

Never let your failures go to your heart or your successes go to your head.
-Soichiro Honda, Japanese engineer, industrialist

Failure is a success if we learn from it.

-Malcolm Forbes, American entrepreneur, publisher of Forbes magazine

Failure is the tuition you pay for success.
-Walter Brunell

I feel the most important requirement to success is learning to overcome failure. You must learn to tolerate it, but never accept it.
-Reggie Jackson, retired American baseball player

Don't let your success of today lay you into complacency for tomorrow. For that is the worst form of failure.
-Og Mandino, American author

Success requires no explanations, failure permits no alibis.
-Napoleon Hill, American author

Persistent people begin their success where others end in failure.
-Edward Eggleston, American historian, novelist

Failure is the foundation of success, and the means by which it is achieved.
-Lao Tzu, Ancient China philosopher, poet

You cannot have any success unless you can accept failure.
-George Cukor, American film director

Success doesn't make you and failure doesn't break you.
-Zig Ziglar, American author, salesman, motivational speaker

Yesterday's failures are today's seeds that must be diligently planted to be able to abundantly harvest tomorrow's success.
-unknown source

The only difference between success and failure is the ability to take action.
-Alexander Graham Bell, Scottish-born scientist, inventor, engineer, innovator

The most vital test of a man's character is not how he behaves after success, but how he sustains defeat.
-Raymond Moley, American presidential adviser, author, professor of law

Success, or failure, very often arrives on wings that seem mysterious to us.
-Dr. Marcus Bach, American philosopher, teacher, minister, author, lecturer
A minute of success pays for years of failure.
-Robert Browning, English poet, playwright

Failure is instructive. The person who really thinks, learns just as much from his failures as he does from his successes.
-John Dewey, American philosopher, psychologist, activist, educational reformer

Success depends upon our previous preparations, and without such preparations there is sure to be failure.
-Confucius, Chinese teacher, editor, politician, philosopher

Any fact facing us is not as important as our attitude toward it, for that determines our success or failure.
-Norman Vincent Peale, author, minister

The two hardest things to handle in life are failure and success.
-unknown source

If you have failed, do not worry. You have just cut the way to success.
-unknown source

Failure doesn't mean that we are off the track to success. It merely forces us to take a detour to success.
-unknown source

Failure is not the only punishment for laziness; there is also the success of others.
-Jules Renard, French author

If one asks for success and prepares for failure, he will get the situation he has prepared for.
-Florence Scovel Shinn, American artist, book illustrator, spiritual teacher

Apparent failure may hold in its rough shell the germs of a success that will bloom in time, and bear fruit throughout eternity.
-Frances Watkins Harper, African-American abolitionist, poet, author

A thinker sees his own actions as experiments and questions - as attempts to find out something. Success and failure are for him answers above all.
-Friedrich Nietzsche, German philosopher, cultural critic, poet, composer

If you are willing to accept failure and learn from it, if you are willing to consider failure as a blessing in disguise and bounce back, you have got the essential of harnessing one of the most powerful success forces.
-Joseph Sugarman, author, internet marketer, copywriting expert

One must be a god to be able to tell successes from failures without making a mistake.
-Anton Chekhov, Russian physician, author

It is a mistake to suppose that men succeed through success; they much oftener succeed through failures. Precept, study, advice, and example could never have taught them so well as failure has done.
-Samuel Smiles, Scottish author, government reformer

If the truth be known, most successes are built on a multitude of failures.
-unknown source

No matter how hard you work for success if your thought is saturated with the fear of failure, it will kill your efforts, neutralize your endeavors and make success impossible.
-Charles Baudouin, French-Swiss psychoanalyst

Don't be discouraged by a failure. It can be a positive experience. Failure is, in a sense, the highway to success, in as much as every discovery of what else leads us to seek earnestly after what is true, and every fresh experience points out some form of error which we shall afterwards carefully avoid.
-John Keats, English romantic poet

If I had permitted my failures, or what seemed to me at the time a lack of success, to discourage me I cannot see any way in which I would ever have made progress.
-Calvin Coolidge, 30th U.S. President

Champions know that success is inevitable that there is no such thing as failure, only feedback. They know that the best way to forecast the future is create it.
-Michael J. Gelb, writer, speaker, personal development expert

Good people are good because they've come to wisdom through failure. We get very little wisdom from success, you know.
-William Saroyan, American dramatist, author

A failure establishes only this, that our determination to succeed was not strong enough.
-John Christian Bovee, author

The saddest failures in life are those that come from not putting forth the power and will to succeed.
-Edwin Whipple, American essayist, critic

You always pass failure on the way to success.
-Mickey Rooney, American actor

The secret of success is this: there is no secret to success.
-Elbert Hubbard, American writer, publisher, artist, philosopher

When they believe in themselves they have the first secret of success.

-Norman Vincent Peale, author, minister

There are no secrets to success. It is the result of preparation, hard work, and learning from failure.
-Colin Powell, American statesman, retired, U.S. Army four-star general

One of the most important keys to success is having the discipline to do what you know you should do, even when you don't feel like doing it.
-unknown source

The whole secret of a successful life is to find out what is one's destiny to do, and then do it.
-Henry Ford, American industrialist, the founder of the Ford Motor Company

The first step toward success is taken when you refuse to be a captive of the environment in which you first find yourself.
-Mark Caine, American climate scientist

Take up one idea. Make that one idea your life - think of it, dream of it, live on that idea. Let the brain, muscles, nerves, every part of your body, be full of that idea, and just leave every other idea alone. This is the way to success.
-Swami Vivekananda, Indian Hindu monk

The path to success is to take massive, determined action.
-Tony Robbins, American life coach, self-help author

One never learns by success. Success is the plateau that one rests upon to take breath and look down from upon the straight and difficult path, but one does not climb upon a plateau.
-Josephine Preston Peabody, American poet, dramatist

There are only two rules for being successful. One, figure out exactly what you want to do, and two, do it.
-Mario Cuomo, American politician

Most people are searching for a path to success that is both easy and certain. Most paths are neither.
-Seth Godin, American author, entrepreneur, marketer, public speaker

Success is not the key to happiness. Happiness is the key to success. If you love what you are doing, you will be successful.
-Albert Schweitzer, OM, German theologian, philosopher, physician, medical missionary in Africa

Action is the foundational key to all success.

-Pablo Picasso, Spanish artist, poet, playwright

Put your heart, mind, and soul into even your smallest acts. This is the secret of success.
-Swami Sivananda, Hindu spiritual teacher, proponent of Yoga

The elevator to success is out of order. You'll have to use the stairs...one step at a time.
-Joe Girard, American salesman

Success is a staircase, not a doorway.
-Dottie Walters, author, speaker

The road to success is dotted with many tempting parking places.
-Will Rogers, American motion picture actor, humorist, social commentator

Create your own path to success, and know that if you're the only one walking it, you must find the way!
-unknown source

The real secret of success is enthusiasm.
-Walter Chrysler, American automotive industry executive, founder of Chrysler Corporation

Success is neither a high jump nor a long jump; it is the steps of a marathon.
-unknown source

It takes the hammer of persistence to drive the nail of success.
-John Mason

One of the most important principles of success is developing the habit of going the extra mile.
-Napoleon Hill, American author

Success is a journey...not a destination.
-Ben Sweetland, author

The secret of success is to never let down and never let up.
-unknown source

If A is a success in life, then A equals x plus y plus z. Work is x; y is play; and z is keeping your mouth shut.
-Albert Einstein, German-born theoretical physicist

I can give you a six-word formula for success: Think things through, then follow through.
-Captain Edward V. Rickenbacker, American fighter ace in World War I, Medal of Honor recipient

As you climb the ladder of success, check occasionally to make sure it is leaning against the right wall.
-unknown source

Success is a ladder you cannot climb with your hands in your pockets.
-Arnold Schwarzenegger, Austrian-born American actor, former professional bodybuilder, politician

The secret of success is to know something nobody else knows.
-Aristotle Onassis, Greek prominent shipping magnate

One important key to success is self confidence. An important key to self confidence is preparation.
-Arthur Ashe, American World No. 1 professional tennis player

Decision and determination are the engineer and fireman of our train to opportunity and success.
-Burt Lawlor, author

If you want to succeed, you should strike out on new paths rather than travel the worn paths of accepted success.
-John D. Rockefeller, American business magnate, philanthropist

There are no speed limits on the road to success.
-David W. Johnson, social psychologist

The first and most important step toward success is the feeling that we can succeed.
-Nelson Boswell, author

Six essential qualities are the key to success: sincerity, personal integrity, humility, courtesy, wisdom, charity.
-William Menninger, psychiatrist

To follow, without halt, one aim: That's the secret of success.
-Anna Pavlova, Russian prima ballerina

Self-trust is the first secret of success.
-Ralph Waldo Emerson, 19th century American essayist, lecturer, and poet

The secret to success is to be ready when opportunity comes.
-Benjamin Disraeli, British Prime Minister, conservative politician, writer

If you can't find the key to success, pick the lock.
-unknown source

Success is the prize for those who stand true to their ideas.
-John S. Hinds

I know the price of success: dedication, hard work, and an unremitting devotion to the things you want to see happen.
-Frank Lloyd Wright, American architect, interior designer, writer, educator

The secret of all success is to know how to deny yourself. Prove that you can control yourself, and you are an educated man; and without this all other education is good for nothing.
-R.D. Hitchcock, American congregationalist clergyman

A great secret of success is to go through life as a man who never gets used up.
-Albert Schweitzer, OM, German theologian, philosopher, physician, medical missionary in Africa

The secret of success is to do all you can do without thought of success.
-unknown source

Your mind, which is yourself, can be likened to a house. The first necessary move then, is to rid that house of all but furnishings essential to success.
-John McDonald, American former professional baseball

The thermometer of success is merely the jealousy of the malcontents.
-Salvador Dali, Spanish surrealist painter

No rules for success will work if you don't.
-unknown source

Strive not to be a success, but rather to be of value.
-Albert Einstein, German-born theoretical physicist

I attribute my success to this: I never gave or took any excuse.
-Florence Nightingale, English social reformer, founder of modern nursing

Eighty percent of success is showing up.
-Woody Allen, American actor, writer, director, comedian, playwright

The best revenge is massive success.
-Frank Sinatra, American singer, actor, director, producer

Success consists of doing the common things of life uncommonly well.
-George Washington Carver, American botanist, inventor

Success seems to be connected with action. Successful people keep moving. They make mistakes but don't quit.
-Conrad Hilton, American hotelier, founder of the Hilton Hotels chain

Success is a state of mind. If you want success, start thinking of yourself as a success.
-Dr. Joyce Brothers, American psychologist, television personality, columnist

Without self-discipline, success is impossible, period.
-Lou Holtz, college football analyst, former football coach

Some people dream of success while others wake up and work hard at it.
-Sir Winston Churchill, British politician, Prime Minister

So long as there is breath in me, that long will I persist. For now I know one of the greatest principles of success; If I persist long enough I will win.
-Og Mandino, American author

Success and rest don't sleep together.
-Russian proverb

Success is 99% attitude and 1% aptitude.
-Celestine Chua, personal development expert, author

Talent is cheaper than table salt. What separates the talented individual from the successful one is a lot of hard work.
-Stephen King, novelist, screenwriter, film director

No one is going to hand me success. I must go out and get it myself. That's why I'm here. To dominate. To conquer. Both the world, and myself.
-unknown source

There is only one success: to be able to spend your life in your own way.
-Christopher Morley, American journalist, novelist, essayist, poet

Success is the sum of small efforts, repeated day in and day out.
-Robert Collier, American author of self-help books

One man has enthusiasm for 30 minutes, another for 30 days, but it is the man who has it for 30 years who makes a success of his life.
-Edward B. Butler, American businessman

The distance between insanity and genius is measured only by success.
-Bruce Feirstein, American screenwriter, humorist

Success is liking yourself, liking what you do, and liking how you do it.
-Maya Angelou, American author, poet, dancer, actress, singer

The successful warrior is the average man with laser-like focus.
-Bruce Lee, actor, martial arts expert, philosopher

Successful people do what unsuccessful people are not willing to do. Don't wish it were easier, wish you were better.
-Jim Rohn, American entrepreneur, author, motivational speaker

The difference between a successful person and others is not a lack of strength, not a lack of knowledge, but rather a lack of will.
-Vince Lombardi, American football player, coach, and executive

Successful and unsuccessful people do not vary greatly in their abilities. They vary in their desires to reach their potential.
-John C. Maxwell, American author, speaker, pastor

It is our attitude at the beginning of a difficult task which, more than anything else, will affect its successful outcome.
-William James, American philosopher and psychologist

The only thing that ever sat its way to success was a hen.
-Sarah Brown, American actress

You don't have to be perfect in order to be successful.
-unknown source

Success isn't a result of spontaneous combustion. You must set yourself on fire.
-Arnold H. Glasow, American author

If you never give up, you'll be successful
-Dan O'Brien, American athlete, 1996 Olympic gold medalist

One's best success comes after their greatest disappointments.
-Henry Ward Beecher, American Congregationalist clergyman, social reformer, speaker

Achieve success in any area of life by identifying the optimum strategies and repeating them until they become habits.
-Charles Givens, American author

Success is the person who year after year, reaches the highest limits in his field.
-Sparky Anderson, Major League Baseball player, manager

A powerful combination to ensure success is having the vision of an eagle and the heart of a lion.
-Robert G. Allen, American author, speaker

Every success is built on the ability to do better than good enough. Nothing great was ever achieved without enthusiasm.
-Ralph Waldo Emerson, 19th century American essayist, lecturer, and poet

Don't aim for success if you want it; just do what you love and believe in, and it will come naturally.
-David Frost, English journalist, comedian, writer, media personality, television host

Opportunity is just success looking for a place to happen.
-Greg Hickman, American businessman, online entrepreneur

Success is the progressive realization of a worthy goal or ideal.
-Earl Nightingale, American self-help speaker, author

Success without honor is an unseasoned dish; it will satisfy your hunger, but it won't taste good.
-Joe Paterno, American college football player, coach

The common denominator for success is work.
-John D. Rockefeller, American business magnate, philanthropist

Success has nothing to do with what you gain in life or accomplish for yourself. It's what you do for others.
-Danny Thomas, American nightclub comedian, actor, producer

He has achieved success who has worked well, laughed often, and loved much.
-Elbert Hubbard, American writer, publisher, artist, philosopher

Success doesn't happen. It is organized, preempted, captured, by consecrated common sense.
-Frances E. Willard, American educator, temperance reformer, women's suffragist

You do not pay the price of success, you enjoy the price of success.
-Zig Ziglar, American author, salesman, motivational speaker

If you can lay your head on your pillow each night knowing you gave hundred per cent to your day, success will find you.
-Russell L. Mason

The more you love what you are doing, the more successful it will be for you.
-Jerry Gillies, American author

Without continual growth and progress, such words as improvement, achievement, and success have no meaning.
-Benjamin Franklin, one of the Founding Fathers of the U.S.

We must never be afraid to go too far, for success lies just beyond.
-Marcel Proust, French novelist, critic, essayist

Success isn't magic or hocus-pocus - it's simply learning how to focus.
-Jack Canfield, American author, motivational speaker

Decide what is worthwhile and follow through with it. Real success is finding your life work in the work that you love.
-David McCullough, American author, narrator, historian, lecturer

Integrity is the essence of everything successful.
-Buckminster Fuller, American neo-futuristic architect, systems theorist, author, inventor

Success is getting what you want. Happiness is wanting what you get.
-Dale Carnegie, American writer, lecturer

It takes time to succeed because success is merely the natural reward of taking time to do anything well.
-Joseph Ross, writer, poet

Success is not measured by what one brings, but rather by what one leaves.
-unknown author

Optimism is the one quality more associated with success and happiness than any other.
-Brian Tracy, American author, motivational speaker

Success is not all about money. It's about having the resources and the ability to live the life that you have personally dreamed of.
-Pete Zafra, blogger, entrepreneur, internet marketer

Success as I see it is a result, not a goal.
-Gustave Flaubert, French writer

Material success may result in the accumulation of possessions; but only spiritual success will enable you to enjoy them.
-Nido Qubein, businessman, motivational speaker

Confidence is the companion of success.
-unknown source

Your chances of success are directly proportional to the degree of pleasure you desire from what you do. If you are in a job you hate, face the fact squarely and get out.
-Michael Korda, English-born writer, novelist

The first principle of success is desire - knowing what you want. Desire is the planting of your seed.
-Robert Collier, American author of self-help books

No one can cheat you out of ultimate success but yourself.
-Ralph Waldo Emerson, 19th century American essayist, lecturer, and poet

Success in the end erases all the mistakes along the way.
-Chinese Proverb

Success is always temporary. When all is said and done, the only thing you'll have left is your character.
-Vince Gill, American country singer-songwriter

Many of us spend our lives searching for success when it is usually so close that we can reach out and touch it.
-Russel H. Conwell, American Baptist minister, orator, philanthropist, lawyer, writer

Never mind what others do; do better than yourself, beat your own record each and everyday, and you are a success.
-William Boetcker, American religious leader, influential public speaker

I couldn't wait for success, so I went ahead without it.
-Jonathan Winter, American comedian, actor, author, artist

I was made to work. If you are equally industrious, you will be equally successful.
-Johann Sebastian Bach, German composer, musician of the Baroque period

Promise yourself to be just as enthusiastic about the success of others as you are about your own.
-Christian Larson, American author

Make a success of living by seeing the goal and aiming at it unswervingly.
-Cecil B. DeMille, American film director, film producer

People begin to become successful the minute they decide to be.
-Harvey MacKay, famous businessman, author and syndicated columnist

Success will not lower its standard to us. We must raise our standard to success.

-Rev. Randall R. McBride, Jr.

I can't imagine a person becoming a success who doesn't give this game of life everything he's got.
-Walter Cronkite, American broadcast journalist

Honesty is the cornerstone of all success, without which confidence and ability to perform shall cease to exist.
-Mary Kay Ash, American businesswoman, founder of Mary Kay Cosmetics, Inc.

The most absurd and reckless aspirations have sometimes led to extraordinary success.
-Luc de Clapiers, minor French writer, moralist

Life is a succession of moments, to live each one is to succeed.
-Coretta Scott King, American author, activist, civil rights leader

All you need in this life is ignorance and confidence; then success is sure.
-Mark Twain, American author, humorist

Always aim for achievement, and forget about success.
-Helen Hayes, American actress

If your success is not on your own terms, if it looks good to the world but does not feel good in your heart, it is not success at all.
-Anna Quindlen, Pulitzer Prize-winning American author, journalist, opinion columnist

The penalty of success is to be bored by people who used to snub you.
-Nancy Astor, American-born English socialite

If you wish success in life, make perseverance your bosom friend, experience your wise counselor, caution your elder brother and hope your guardian genius.
-Joseph Addison, English essayist, poet, playwright, politician

There are people who make things happen, there are people who watch things happen, and there are people who wonder what happened. To be successful, you need to be a person who makes things happen.
-James Lovell, former NASA astronaut, retired U.S. Navy captain

Aim for success, not perfection. Never give up your right to be wrong, because then you will lose the ability to learn new things and move forward with your life.
-Dr. David M. Burns, psychiatrist, author

Success in life is measured, most easily, by the number of days that a person is truly happy.
-Eric Edmeades, Editor, Success Express Journal (circa 1996)

Mental toughness is essential to success.
-Vince Lombardi, American football player, coach, and executive

Success: Set your standards high, and do not stop till you reach them.
-Bo Jackson, retired American baseball, football player

Success is a science; if you have the conditions, you get the result.
-Oscar Wilde, Irish writer and poet

No one can possibly achieve any real and lasting success or "get rich" in business by being a conformist.
-J. Paul Getty, American industrialist, 1966 World Guinness Record

Holder as world's richest private citizen

Success is more a function of consistent common sense than it is of genius.
-An Wang, Chinese American computer engineer and inventor

Successful men follow the same advice they prescribe for others.
-unknown source

One essential to success is that your desire be an all-obsessing one, your thoughts and aims be coordinated, and your energy be concentrated and applied without letup.
-Claude M. Bristol, author

Are the things around you helping you toward success - or are they holding you back?
-Clement Stone, American businessman, philanthropist, author

If you want to be truly successful invest in yourself to get the knowledge you need to find your unique factor. When you find it and focus on it and persevere your success will blossom.
-Sidney Madwed, American speaker, poet, lyricist, author

Experience shows that success is due less to ability than to zeal. The winner is he who gives himself to his work, body and soul.
-Charles Buxton, English brewer, philanthropist, writer, member of Parliament

If you achieve success, you will get applause, and if you get applause, you will hear it. My advice to you concerning applause is this; enjoy it but never quite believe it.
-Robert Montgomery, American actor, director, producer

Success, in a generally accepted sense of the term, means the opportunity to experience and to realize to the maximum the forces that are within us.

-David Sarnoff, American businessman, pioneer of American radio and television

Make service your first priority, not success and success will follow.
-unknown source

Every success is built on the ability to do better than good enough.
-unknown source

You have reached the pinnacle of success as soon as you become uninterested in money, compliments, or publicity.
-Thomas Wolfe, American novelist

Success is peace of mind which is a direct result of self-satisfaction in knowing you did your best to become the best you are capable of becoming.
-John Wooden, American basketball player, coach

Pray that success will not come any faster than you are able to endure it.
-Benjamin Nnamdi Azikiwe, one of the leading figures of modern Nigerian nationalism

My success just evolved from working hard at the business at hand each day.
-Johnny Carson, American television host, comedian, writer, producer

No one ever excused his way to success.
-Dave Del Dotto, author, former real estate investor

Hard work doesn't guarantee success, but improves its chances.
-B. J. Gupta, author

The true measure of your worth includes all the benefits others have gained from your success.
-Cullen Hightower, American quotation, quip writer

The gent who wakes up and finds himself a success hasn't been asleep.
-Wilson Mizner, American playwright, raconteur, entrepreneur

If you want to be successful, find someone who has achieved the results you want and copy what they do and you'll achieve the same results.
-Tony Robbins, American life coach, self-help author

Money and success don't change people they merely amplify what is already there.
-Will Smith, American actor, producer, rapper, songwriter

A man can succeed at almost anything for which he has unlimited enthusiasm.
-Charles Schwab, American businessman, investor

There is no point at which you can say, "Well I am successful now, I might as well relax."
-Carrie Fisher, American actress, novelist, screenwriter, performance artist

My Gratitude & Contact Info

Thank you for downloading our book. We hope you enjoyed it and found many insightful things.

We're not all about selling you books—We do want to see you use what you've learned to build a greater life. As you work toward your goals, however, you may have questions or run into some issues. We'd like to be able to help you, so let's connect. We don't charge for the assistance, so feel free to connect through any of the facets below:

On the web:

BootstrapBusinessmen.com

Like us on Facebook:

http://www.facebook.com/bootstrapbusinessmen

Follow us on Twitter:

http://www.twitter.com/bootstrapbiz

Follow us on Instagram:

http://www.instagram.com/bootstrapbusinessmen

Thank you, again! I hope to hear from you and wish you the best.

-Bootstrap Businessmen

Additional Resources

Brainy Quotes - www.brainyquote.com/

Goodreads - http://www.goodreads.com/quotes

Pinterest - https://www.pinterest.com/categories/quotes/

Quoteland - www.quoteland.com/

Jim Rohn - www.jimrohn.com/

John C. Maxwell - www.johnmaxwell.com/

Les Brown - lesbrown.com/

Quoteland - www.quoteland.com

World of Quotes - www.worldofquotes.com

Tony Robbins - www.tonyrobbins.com/

Dr. Wayne Dyer - http://www.drwaynedyer.com/

Napoleon Hill - http://www.naphill.org/

Quotabl.es - https://quotabl.es/

www.ingramcontent.com/pod-product-compliance
Lightning Source LLC
Chambersburg PA
CBHW062020280526
45787CB00005B/2175